FIRST PEOPLES OF NORTH AMERICA

THE PEOPLE AND CULTURE OF THE

CREE

RAYMOND BIAL

Cavendish
Square

New York

Published in 2016 by Cavendish Square Publishing, LLC
243 5th Avenue, Suite 136, New York, NY 10016

Copyright © 2016 by Cavendish Square Publishing, LLC

First Edition

Website: cavendishsq.com

This publication represents the opinions and views of the author based on his or her personal experience, knowledge, and research. The information in this book serves as a general guide only. The author and publisher have used their best efforts in preparing this book and disclaim liability rising directly or indirectly from the use and application of this book.

CPSIA Compliance Information: Batch #CW16CSQ

All websites were available and accurate when this book was sent to press.

Library of Congress Cataloging-in-Publication Data

Bial, Raymond.
[Cree.]
The people and culture of the Cree / Raymond Bial.
pages cm. — (First peoples of North America)
Includes bibliographical references and index.
ISBN 978-1-5026-0998-4 (hardcover) ISBN 978-1-5026-0999-1 (ebook)
1. Cree Indians—History—Juvenile literature. 2. Cree Indians—Social life and customs—Juvenile literature. I. Title.
E99.C88B55 2016
971.2004'97323—dc23

2015023311

Editorial Director: David McNamara
Editor: Kristen Susienka
Copy Editor: Nathan Heidelberger
Art Director: Jeffrey Talbot
Designer: Amy Greenan
Senior Production Manager: Jennifer Ryder-Talbot
Production Editor: Renni Johnson
Photo Research: J8 Media

Printed in the United States of America

ACKNOWLEDGMENTS

A number of individuals and organizations helped in the photography, research, and writing for *The People and Culture of the Cree*. I would like to acknowledge the wonderful people in Chisasibi near James Bay in northern Quebec. I would especially like to thank Sam Cox, who kindly guided me through the ancestral homeland of his people. My days with Sam were among the very best of my life.

I am again very thankful to Cavendish Square Publishing for overseeing this book through editing to production. As always, I would like to express my deepest appreciation to my wife, Linda, and my children Anna, Sarah, and Luke, who have long provided such a wellspring of inspiration.

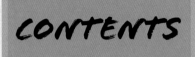

CONTENTS

A mother and child sit inside a tipi, waiting for a ceremony called Walking Out to begin.

AUTHOR'S NOTE

At the dawn of the twentieth century, Native Americans were thought to be a vanishing race. However, despite four hundred years of warfare, deprivation, and disease, Native Americans have persevered. Countless thousands have lost their lives, but over the course of this century and the last, the populations of Native tribes have grown tremendously. Even as America's First People struggle to adapt to modern Western life, they have also kept the flame of their traditions alive—the languages, religions, stories, and the everyday ways of life. An exhilarating renaissance in Native American culture is now sweeping the continent from coast to coast.

The First Peoples of North America books depict the social and cultural life of the major nations, from the early history of Native peoples in North America to their present-day struggles for survival and dignity. Historical and contemporary photographs of traditional subjects, as well as period illustrations, are blended throughout each book so that readers may gain a sense of family life in a tipi, a hogan, or a longhouse.

No single book can comprehensively portray the intricate and varied lifeways of an entire tribe, or nation. I only hope that young people will come away with a deeper appreciation for the rich tapestry of Native American culture—both then and now—and a keen desire to learn more about these first Americans.

Hudson Bay and James Bay (to the south) have been home to the Cree for centuries.

CHAPTER ONE

Life in the bush remains central to the identity of the Cree.

—photographer Louise Abbott

A CULTURE BEGINS

For centuries, many Cree have called the James Bay area in Quebec, Canada, home. Today, there are several branches of the Cree Nation. They still remain on some of the lands their ancestors settled, near James Bay and elsewhere in Canada. This group of Native people has a remarkable story that dates back thousands of years. The Cree first settled the area around James Bay more than six thousand years ago. There they built houses and established communities. Family groups created units called tribes. They lived in relative isolation until European settlers arrived in the seventeenth century, changing their lives and society forever.

The Cree's Creation Story

Having no written language, the Cree's earliest ancestors relied on storytelling and oral tradition to keep their history and culture alive. Stories still have great power in present-day Cree communities. One of the best-preserved stories is about the creation of the world:

> At one time, long ago, the earth was covered with water. Floating upon the surface of the water, the animals longed for dry land. The muskrat offered to dive down and try to bring up some mud. He plunged deep into the water but barely reached the bottom. He returned to the surface, gasping for air. On his skinny tail, he carried a little mud, but it was not enough. The bit of mud immediately sank back to the bottom. Then the otter dove down to the bottom, but he too failed to bring back enough mud on his slender tail. Finally, the beaver tried. He was gone for a very long time. All the other animals thought that he surely must have drowned. However, at last the beaver popped to the surface. He was exhausted, but the other animals saw that there was enough mud on his broad, flat tail to form a small island. And from this island the world grew.

Cree artist and sculptor Don McLeay explains to a group of schoolchildren the story of how the beaver got its tail.

How the Cree Began

The ancestors of the Cree have lived in Canada for at least 6,500 years. Related by language and culture, the Cree occupied an enormous territory—from north-central Quebec in the east all the way to the Rocky Mountains of western Canada. With many tribes and bands, the Cree were one of North America's largest Native groups. Their language was—and still is—one of the most widely spoken Native languages in North America. "Cree" comes from the Ojibwe name for a member of this tribe, *Kenishteno*, translated into French as *Kristineaux* and shortened to *Kris* or *Kri* (pronounced "kree"). Crees refer to themselves with the term Cree when speaking English, but in their own language they call themselves by other terms, such as *Iyiniwak*, meaning "People," and *Nehiyawak*, meaning "Those who speak the same language."

The Cree are traditionally divided into several groups, each speaking its own variety of the Cree language. Beginning in the east are the East Main Cree, or East Cree, south and east of Hudson Bay in the Canadian province of Quebec. East Cree living along the bay are said to be Coasters, while those who live inland are called Inlanders.

Just to the west are the West Main Cree, also called Muskegon or Swampy Cree, whose homeland is south and west of Hudson Bay. The West Main Cree have ten regional subdivisions: Abitibi, Albany, Attawapiskat, Monsoni, Moose River (or Moose Cree), Nipigon, Piscontagami, Severn, Winish, and Winnipeg.

Farther west are the Western Woods Cree, or Woodland Cree, who make their home in the northern portions of three Canadian provinces: Manitoba, Saskatchewan, and Alberta. They have three major subdivisions: Rocky Cree, Western Swampy Cree, and Strongwoods Cree.

South of the Western Woods Cree are the Plains Cree, who migrated onto the prairies of Saskatchewan in the 1700s. There they adopted many customs of the Plains tribes. The name Saskatchewan itself comes from a Cree word meaning "swift flowing river."

The early Cree were feared and respected as a powerful tribe living in a vast territory east of the Hudson and James Bays and as far west as Alberta and the Great Slave Lake. Because of their many friendships with other Native people, the Cree could freely move from one band to another and could also marry outside their tribe. By the sixteenth century, when Europeans began arriving, there were at least twenty thousand Cree people. As the fur trade developed, the Cree became the hub of the largest alliance of tribes in North America.

Their traditional allies included the Assiniboine, the Blackfeet Confederacy (before 1800), and the Ojibwe, whom the Cree regarded as their cousins. Their enemies included the Blackfeet (after 1800), the Gros Ventre, Iroquois, Dakota, Inuit, and the western Athapaskan tribes.

The Cree became involved in the fur trade not long after Europeans began to explore North America. The Cree first encountered Europeans when Henry Hudson explored their territory around James Bay in 1611. He brought a knife, a mirror, and some buttons that he traded for two beaver pelts. Great Britain and France, which claimed parts of Cree territory, looked for ways to acquire furs—especially beaver pelts—from Canada to satisfy the demands of fashionable Europeans. In 1670, the Hudson's Bay Company was established under British authority at the mouth of the Nelson River. This company claimed trading rights to all the land that drained into Hudson Bay. This area in Cree territory became known as Rupert's Land.

Accustomed to the rugged terrain and often extreme weather, the Cree were well suited to be trappers and traders. They made long journeys by birch-bark canoes in warm weather and by toboggan and birch-frame snowshoes in the winter. They quickly

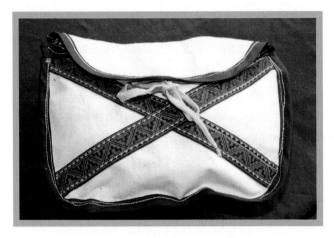

Women made and decorated beautiful clothing, shoes, and pouches like this one.

developed good relationships with the newcomers, who offered brass kettles, steel traps, rifles, blankets, cloth, and glass beads, along with metal knives, axes, scrapers, and fishhooks in exchange for animal pelts.

The British and French continued to set up trading posts in Cree country from 1690 to 1740. Intense demand for furs then prompted France to send traders westward to exchange goods with the Cree and other tribes. Beginning in the mid-eighteenth century, forts were established farther west.

Moreover, French and British trappers and traders who ventured into the wilderness of North America became very skilled in wilderness survival. They also came to appreciate Native women, especially Cree women. These remarkable women could hunt game, catch fish, gather foods, prepare meals, make snowshoes, and sew clothing, including **moccasins**. British and French traders and trappers, known as voyageurs, began to live with or marry these women, which helped them form alliances with Cree bands.

Cree leaders encouraged these marriages, which assured that trade goods would be available and that there would be a steady market for their furs. The children of these marriages came to be called **Métis**, which is the French term for "mixed blood." The Métis often became skilled hunters and trappers. Since they could speak both Cree and French, they also became valuable guides and interpreters in the fur trade. Over time, they developed their own culture.

The Cree had been trading with other tribes in the forests and on the plains long before the first trading forts were established in their territory. By controlling the rivers, lakes, and trails, they could help or hamper other tribes that tried to visit the trading posts. Trading became so vital to the Cree that they began to serve as "middlemen" between the Europeans and other Native bands. They often played the French and British against each other—raiding the French posts in the south and the British posts in the north. They acquired firearms from the Hudson's Bay Company and completed an

Cree men and women wore moccasins like these.

alliance with the Assiniboine, which allowed the Cree to expand almost to the Arctic Sea, the Rocky Mountains, and the Red River. Living near the trading posts, they swapped for European goods, which they traded to tribes living farther inland, returning with prime furs that they exchanged for more goods from the French and British. They dominated the region from the Eastmain River to the Winnipeg River and monopolized trade with the Hudson's Bay Company, which set up trading posts between 1670 and 1688 at the mouths of the Nelson, Moose, and Albany Rivers.

In fact, Cree became the most commonly used language in the fur trade. At the same time, however, the Cree also became dependent on traders for cloth, blankets, tools, weapons, and other necessities. They no longer made their own tools and weapons. Cloth replaced buckskin in making clothing. People also wanted new foods, such as flour and sugar, along with tobacco and alcohol. They began to devote much of their energy to trapping and trading furs for goods of European manufacture instead of hunting, fishing, and gathering.

By the 1760s, France was losing its territory in North America. The French posts closed, and competition between British and French fur buyers ended. Eventually, in 1821, the Hudson's Bay Company and another British trading company, the North West Company, merged to become the largest and most powerful fur-trading company in the world. The Hudson's Bay Company dominated nearly all the territory in Canada for many years—until 1870, when the title was transferred to the Canadian government.

The People and Culture of the Cree

However, while the Hudson's Bay Company prospered, the fur trade was becoming less beneficial to the Cree. When the beaver and other fur-bearing animals in their Native territory had been trapped and moose and caribou had been overhunted, many tribes had to move farther west. By the mid-1700s, Cree bands found a new way of life on the **Great Plains**. They adopted many aspects of Plains Native American culture, such as acquiring horses and hunting buffalo. Just as the horse replaced the birch-bark canoe, the buffalo replaced the beaver. It had the advantage of providing most of the Cree's needs for food, clothing, and shelter, along with many tools and household items. Having acquired horses by the mid-eighteenth century, the Plains Cree traveled great distances over the western prairies. By 1845, a Plains Cree tribe was firmly established in the West.

The Environment

East Main Cree people, both Coasters and Inlanders, live in an extensive lowland east of James Bay. This territory includes sweeping beaches, islands, and rivers branching through boggy land known as **muskeg**. The swamps are studded with wild flowers and grasses such as arrowheads, blue flag irises, and cattails. The still waters are surrounded by forests of black spruce and shrubs, such as speckled alder, Labrador tea, and late low blueberry. Sedges thrive in the damp environment, and the floor of the thin forests is blanketed with mosses including feather, hair cap, and sphagnum.

This swampy land has long supported sizable populations of big game, such as caribou, moose, and black bears. Beavers, otters, lynx, and rabbits were also hunted or trapped by the Cree. Game birds, such as spruce grouse and ptarmigan, inhabited the forests, while flocks of ducks and geese flew overhead in seasonal migrations. In the coastal waters, the Cree occasionally hunted polar bears, seals, and beluga whales. They also caught many kinds of fish, including cisco, whitefish, trout, sturgeon, and pike.

During the summer, the Coasters camped along the shore and river mouths to keep away from the spongy muskeg, which bred clouds of biting insects. During the colder months, they trudged along trails in snowshoes to trading posts, while Inlanders paddled canoes along the rivers before the winter freeze.

The West Main Cree, or Swampy Cree, lived in the low-lying region west of James and Hudson Bays, stretching to the Churchill River in northern Manitoba. There the muskeg was laced with many rivers and streams, along which the Cree paddled their canoes or easily **portaged** from one headwater to another. The soggy land was studded with spruce, tamarack, and willow trees, where the Cree hunted moose and caribou. Huge flocks of ducks and geese, making their annual journeys south, darkened the skies in the flyways.

The Western Woods Cree inhabited the thick forests west of the Hudson and James Bays, which included the northern parts of Ontario, Manitoba, Saskatchewan, and Alberta. The forest consisted of white and black spruce, along with conifers, such as tamarack, balsam fir, and jack pine. Broad-leaved trees included white birch, trembling aspen, and balsam poplar. In the lowlands, a forest of black spruce and tamarack gave way to patches of tundra amid a vast number of lakes, rivers, and streams.

There, the Cree hunted elk, wood bison, and white-tailed deer, but woodland caribou and moose were their most important large game. Barren Ground caribou were also hunted if the herds happened to migrate through Cree territory. Black bears were especially sought for rituals. The Cree also hunted small game, such as porcupines, woodchucks, rabbits, and squirrels. They trapped a number of fur-bearing animals, including beavers, muskrats, minks, otters, lynxes, martens, foxes, gray wolves, and wolverines. They hunted ducks and geese and caught many kinds of fish—pike, pickerel, whitefish, and trout.

The Plains Cree originally inhabited the forests between Lake Superior and Hudson Bay. However,

Bison were among the many animals hunted for food and fur.

Many of the Cree's beliefs involved their Creator, who was thought to dwell all around them—in the air, the water, and the sky.

during the eighteenth and nineteenth centuries, bands migrated to the sweeping plains of western Saskatchewan and eastern Alberta, and south to northern Montana. Following the herds of buffalo, they lived farthest north of all the Plains tribes in North America, their range extending into the Canadian Rockies. There, they made a new home for themselves in a landscape of rolling plains, and they faced brutally cold winters, especially when arctic winds plunged down from the north.

The People and Culture of the Cree

A Prevailing People

Wherever they lived, the Cree adapted to the land
and climate and prospered by hunting, fishing, and
gathering. They have proven themselves a hearty
people who persist even when adversity strikes.
Through the centuries, the Cree and their many
branches have endured physical and emotional
hardship, as well as times of peace and tranquility.
The ways these communities formed likewise tested
their mental and physical abilities, encouraging them
to survive against all odds.

Many Cree families lived in tipis, which were covered with bark or animal skins. Newer versions are covered in canvas.

> We Crees ... are the
> peoples of the land ...
> We have always lived here.
>
> —Matthew Coon Come,
> Grand Chief of the Grand
> Council of the Crees

BUILDING A CIVILIZATION

The groups of Cree people that moved west to the Canadian prairies established communities. There they hunted buffalo, constructed homes called **tipis**, and developed a lifestyle similar to that of the Plains people elsewhere in North America. These communities prospered under the guidance and governance of various community members. All people in the community were important to making it function and thrive. This is what was common in many early Cree communities.

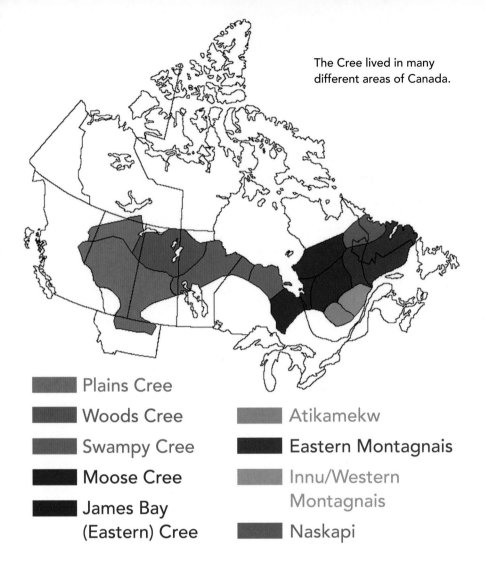

The Cree lived in many different areas of Canada.

- Plains Cree
- Woods Cree
- Swampy Cree
- Moose Cree
- James Bay (Eastern) Cree
- Atikamekw
- Eastern Montagnais
- Innu/Western Montagnais
- Naskapi

The Community

The Cree tribes were loosely composed of several small groups, called bands. These bands lived separately from each other during the colder months but joined together in the summer. While together, they held councils and hosted ceremonies. Among the Cree, people had to be adaptable if they were going to survive in the bush. Men hunted, went on raids, and protected their families. Women were responsible for preserving meat, tanning hides, and watching over children. Yet to survive in the harsh environment, especially through the long winters, men and women also worked together and shared many duties.

Each Cree band was made up of a number of extended families, often including grandparents and unmarried aunts and uncles. They had band leaders and territorial chiefs who were chosen for their merit and spiritual powers. However, these leaders served at the will of the people. After the Cree encountered Europeans, these leaders took charge of trade between their people and the newcomers.

Young people today continue learning ancient Cree traditions and beliefs.

Like other Native people, the Cree highly valued their families. In their large family groups, aunts and uncles often acted as mothers and fathers in teaching and caring for children. Elders were loved and respected as grandmothers and grandfathers. Even distant relatives of one's own age were thought of as cousins, and those of a parent's generation were treated as aunts and uncles. People often looked after the elderly, orphans, and widows who had no family of their own. Relatives also avenged murders and other crimes against family members.

The Cree way of life changed when Europeans arrived and introduced horses.

In the early eighteenth century, the Plains Cree first acquired horses, which completely transformed their way of life. They relied on horses as both pack animals and mounts for travel and hunting. By the 1790s, these canoe-paddling fur trappers had become accomplished horsemen who traveled across the plains, following the herds of buffalo.

Most Plains Cree families owned several horses to carry their belongings whenever they broke camp. A few prestigious men also owned horses that had been specially trained to hunt buffalo. These buffalo horses reflected the wealth and social position of the owner. Men could trade for these valuable mounts, but most often they raided enemy camps and stole them. A horse was considered the best and most honorable gift. When a Plains Cree man died, the manes and tails of his horses were clipped as a sign of respect. If the man had been wealthy, upon his death, his many horses were given to his family and needy families in his band.

Ruling, Raids, and the Warrior Society

Among the Plains Cree, there were between eight and twelve loose, shifting bands named for their territory or chief. Families usually followed a chief known for his prestige and generosity. Except during war, a family could freely leave a band if they were unhappy with the chief. When a chief died, his son often succeeded him. However, although this leadership position was hereditary, an unfit heir could be rejected, and a more worthy man would be chosen. A brave and generous man could then become chief after proving himself as a hunter, warrior, and orator. Each band also had a Warrior Society, which provided leadership.

All Plains Cree warriors achieved prestige through warfare, wealth, and generosity. Young men were encouraged to be brave fighters and skilled hunters. The Plains Cree often raided camps, usually at night—not so much to fight an enemy, but mainly to steal as many horses as possible. Among warriors, a tactic called "counting coup" was as important as killing an enemy. A warrior counted coup by riding up to an armed enemy and touching him with a lance or coup stick. This was more dangerous than shooting an enemy from a distance. It put the warrior directly into contact with the enemy, with the aim of attacking when the enemy least expected it. A warrior who killed an enemy while under fire was more highly esteemed than a man who shot an enemy as part of an ambush.

Bravery in the face of danger mattered most, and men were ranked by their war exploits. The most courageous young fighters were honored as *Okihtchitawak*, or "Worthy Young Men." Some earned this title after their first raid. Others might have had to strive for a long time before they had proved themselves. Worthy Young Men became members of the Warrior Society when they were formally asked to join the group. Individuals who distinguished themselves might someday rise to become chiefs of their bands.

The Warrior Society chose a war chief based on his proven courage and skill in battle. The war chief oversaw the dances and police functions of the Warrior Society. In times of war, he took over the general leadership of the band. Under the leadership of the war chief, the Warrior Society organized the buffalo hunts, making sure no one got too eager and stampeded the herd. The group also established the corrals, known as pounds, into which buffalo were driven, supplied materials for ceremonial lodges, took care of the poor, and enforced law in the camp. Theft and other crimes were rare, and these matters were easily resolved. However, murder triggered blood revenge. If families were caught up in an ongoing dispute, the Warrior Society brought the families together in a tipi and showed them an object called the **Sacred Pipe Stem**. The Cree used the pipe to begin all rituals and social occasions, and they held the pipe stem in such high regard that its presence was usually enough to end a conflict.

Members of the Warrior Society also guarded the line of march when the band moved camp and made sure stragglers were not left behind. Once a warrior became a member, he was not allowed to be jealous, greedy, or afraid. Each Warrior Society had its own songs, dances, and rituals.

This drawing shows a Sacred Pipe Stem.

Resolving Conflict

When an important decision had to be made, a crier summoned the leading men to the chief's tipi. The chief then explained the matter to them. Each man spoke in order of his age and prestige within the band—the youngest first and the highest-ranking man last. This council reached a decision through consensus, meaning that everyone agreed. However, a chief sometimes listened to everyone and then made the decision himself.

Housing

The Cree lived in several kinds of homes: a cone-shaped summer tipi made of thick poles, hide or bark sheathing, and spruce boughs; a dome-shaped **wigwam** covered with birch bark, pine bark, or caribou hides; or a rectangular winter home of logs and sod. People who lived in the southern part of Cree territory usually covered their dwellings with birch bark. Farther north and west, the Cree used sheets of pine bark or animal skins from caribou, elk, or moose. Extended families of ten or more people lived in each dwelling. These dwellings had a single low doorway and a smoke hole at the top. A fire was kept burning in a pit in the center of the floor. However, the larger, rectangular lodges had two fires inside. Covered with thick layers of sod, these dwellings remained warm even on the coldest winter nights.

The Cree tipi was formed around three main poles, instead of the four or more poles used by other tribes. To make the tipi, they first cut cedar or spruce trees and peeled off the bark. About 19 feet (5.8 meters) long, the heavy poles had to be tapered—5 to 8 inches (12.7 to 20.3 centimeters) at the bottom and 2 to 4 inches (5.1 to 10.2 cm) at the top. They tied the three longest poles together about 2 feet (0.6 m) from the top and raised them, spreading out the bottom legs to form a tripod. The builders then laid about thirty poles around this frame, spacing them about 1.5 to 2 feet (0.5 to 0.6 m) apart, except for the doorway, which was about 3 feet (0.9 m) wide. Two longer poles were placed on each side of the doorway, which faced east. These poles slightly extended the eastern side so the tipi was not a true triangle.

Once the poles were set up, the Cree laid fresh cedar or spruce boughs on the floor in a clockwise manner. The boughs overlapped in a circle around a fire pit left open in the center of the tipi. The green boughs provided a soft cushion and gave off a pleasant scent. The Cree then sheathed the tipi with a pie-shaped animal hide covering. They tied a cover for the door and added a

12- to 18-inch-wide (30.5 to 45.7 cm wide) skirt around the bottom of the tipi, which was about 19 feet (5.8 m) in diameter. Horizontal poles were tied across the inside of the tipi from one wall to another. These were used to hang meat and kettles over the fire pit.

In the 1700s, the Plains Cree brought their woodland tipi to the western prairies and began sheathing the lodges with a covering made of buffalo hides. It is believed that the tipi style of other tribes was influenced by the Cree tipi, especially after the Plains tribes acquired horses. Horses could drag much heavier loads on sled-like carriers known as **travois**. Plains tipis then became much larger, often doubling in length. Ten to twelve people could take shelter in a tipi. Made of twelve to twenty buffalo hides, the Plains Cree tipi was not a true cone. Its steeper rear braced the structure against the prevailing westerly winds so that it appeared to be slightly tilted. Its doorway faced the rising sun. Its base was not a true circle but egg-shaped, with the wider end in the back.

The inside of the tipi was also lined with buffalo hides to provide better insulation. Women made the tipi, set it up, and owned it. A man had to ask permission to draw a picture of his **spirit helper** on the inside walls. Inside the tipi there was a fire ring, and smoke rose through an open flap at the top of the structure. On the earthen floor were beds made from bundles of dried grass or rushes over which people laid buffalo robes. Women made pillows by filling rawhide pouches with duck feathers.

Whether they made their home in the forests or on the plains, the Cree respected the living space in their tipis. In early stories, they told of a supernatural woman who traveled ahead of the hunters to set up their tipis and prepare their camp. She did such a good job that no matter where they moved, it seemed as if they were staying in the same place. Children were warned not to count the poles in their tipi or the woman's magic would be lost. Each person within a Cree dwelling also had a particular space where he or she slept—determined by age, sex, family, and marital status. The Cree followed this practice even when they lived in temporary camps. This sleeping arrangement gave each person a little privacy and a feeling that they had their own small space.

Cree camps and villages also had other structures. Band members constructed **sweat lodges** for purifying themselves and curing illnesses. About 4 feet (1.2 m) high and 6 feet (1.8 m) in diameter, these dome-shaped lodges consisted of a wooden framework over which people threw robes and blankets. Heated stones were passed through a hole in the side of the sweat lodge. Water was then poured over the hot stones, and people bathed in the rising steam. Among the Plains Cree, sweetgrass was burned and a pipe was offered in the sweat lodge. The structure was often used in the Sweat Lodge Ceremony and then abandoned. In each village, there were also menstrual lodges (where women retired for a few days each month), grounds for ceremonies, and storage pits known as caches.

Today, most Cree live in modern houses. However, many families still move out into the bush for at least part of the year—for a short hunting trip, a weeklong fishing camp, or an entire season. During the winter,

Cedar trees helped the Cree build shelters, such as tipis.

they may move into a rectangular home of logs and sod called a **muhtukan**. When they move to summer camps, they might live in a tipi called a **michwaup**. These tipis are still made with cedar or spruce poles and boughs, but they are now covered with canvas instead of bark or animal skins.

Over the centuries of their existence, the Cree have kept their traditions and customs alive. Their societies were structured in such a way as to promote protection of their people and equality among men and women. By respecting the earth and all living things, they established connections with the world around them. Today, many Cree continue to follow the example of their ancestors.

A member of the Northern Cree tribe waits for the grand entry at the Red Earth Native American Cultural Festival in Oklahoma City in 1993.

*Love one another and
help one another.*

—Cree proverb

LIFE IN THE CREE NATION

The early Cree lived off the land. They hunted for food, traveled long distances, and built societies over a vast region of Canada. The Cree lifestyle was similar to other Native communities. They valued family, held rituals and ceremonies that celebrated their beliefs, and structured their lives around their environment and resources. They were expert craftspeople who took great care in forming the objects they made. They respected the land and treated it well. Today, the Cree still display many of these characteristics and uphold traditions of the past.

The Stages of Life

The Cree were closely bound to the land and the changing seasons. Their lives revolved around the daily tasks of raising children and preparing meals and the seasonal activities of gathering, fishing, hunting, and trapping. Every spring, they gathered plants in the forest. Every summer, they moved to fishing camps. Every autumn, they trudged on snowshoes to hunt game and run trap lines. As the snows deepened around them, they settled around the fires in their lodges to listen to stories of their ancestors. Just as their lives followed the seasons, from one generation to the next, so did their customs and beliefs regarding the cycle of life from birth, childhood, and coming-of-age to marriage, old age, and death.

Starting Life

When a woman was about to give birth, two or three older, experienced women served as midwives. If the band was on the move, it halted briefly until the baby was born. The newborn was placed in a **cradleboard**, and dried moss was used as a diaper. Among the Plains Cree, the baby also wore a small pouch that held its umbilical cord, which was considered a sacred object. Within a few months, an older person named the baby after an animal, a plant, the seasons, or a certain territory. There was no special naming ceremony. However, if the father had a good hunt, a feast might be held for the infant. Over the years, the child was

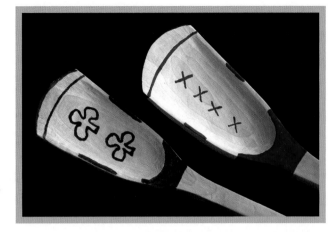

Cree children enjoyed games and toys. Often their mothers and fathers made toys or game pieces from wood.

given other names related to special events and dreams. Babies were sometimes weaned after a year, but usually nursed until they were about three years old. When the child was about to take his or her first steps, the Cree held a Walking Out ceremony. A boy traditionally carried a small wooden gun and a girl held a wooden ax as they took their first steps outside their home in the hope that they would walk upon the earth for many years.

Parents and Children

The Cree cherished family life. Parents were loving and gentle to their children and taught them to respect others. They rarely punished their offspring, preferring to teach by example. During the summer, children played outside, but in the dangerously cold winters they had to be amused inside the tipi.

Parents emphasized practical training for their children. As they grew up, children helped their parents and learned the skills of hunting, fishing, and gathering. Girls were very close to their mothers and aunts, from whom they learned how to take care of the household, cook meals, make clothing, and look after younger brothers and sisters. Fathers and uncles were responsible for teaching the boys. From an early age, boys became skilled with the bow and arrow in hunting and warfare, as well as building and paddling canoes, making rabbit snares, and setting beaver traps. However, since their parents were often busy providing food, clothing, and shelter, children spent a lot of time with their grandparents, with whom they were especially close.

Joining Adulthood

A feast was held for a boy when he killed his first big game. Then, as the young man approached puberty, he went on a **vision quest**. He traveled with his father or grandfather to a secluded place where they made a shelter out of brush. The boy was left alone to fast and pray in the shelter until he had a vision of one or more spirit helpers. These spirits presented him with gifts and rituals that would help him throughout his life. Sometimes, the boy repeated the vision quest to seek more gifts, or if he had been instructed to do so in a previous vision. Men also went on vision quests, but they rarely had visions unless they had first thoroughly purified themselves with a time of fasting.

Young women did not go on vision quests. However, when they had their first menstrual period, and every other time after that, they had to isolate themselves in a special hut away from the band. During their first time of seclusion, young women often had visions and acquired their own spirit helpers, who might give them special powers. One of the greatest gifts that could be received in a vision was the ability to heal the ill and injured. Any man or woman who received this rare gift became a healer, or **shaman**.

These various rituals helped to prepare young people for adulthood. After they had learned all the skills needed for survival, young women and men were ready to marry.

Horses graze in a meadow with a mountain looming in the distance.

Matrimony

Women usually married three or four years after puberty. Men usually married when they were about twenty-five and better able to support a family. When a young man fell in love with a young woman, he followed her for days without talking to her—this was his way of expressing interest in her. If she liked him, she then went home and told her parents. If her parents thought the young man would be a good match for their daughter, the father offered a gift to the young man's father. The young man and woman then sat down together in a new tipi erected by her family. She gave him a pair of moccasins, and if he accepted, the couple was considered to be married. The couple then moved into their own lodge.

Among the Plains Cree, the bride's family presented a fully equipped tipi to the couple. Horses, once they were introduced to the Cree, were a common gift from the father-in-law to the groom. If the parents did not approve of the match, the couple eloped. They ran away together and settled down with another tribe. After a while, they returned to their parents, who usually accepted the couple and their marriage. Parents sometimes arranged marriages to strengthen an alliance between bands or tribes. If a couple did not get along, they separated, with either the man or the woman returning to a parent's tipi. After a while, they were free to marry again.

Rituals of the Dead

A dying person was dressed in his finest clothing. His face was painted, and his pipe was prepared. The man then made his last requests to his family: to whom his property should be given and how his survivors should avenge his death. The Cree believed that witchcraft practiced by an enemy caused illness, so revenge had to be taken. As soon as the man died, a rifle was fired to keep the spirit of death from returning to the lodge.

The body was wrapped in bark, then either buried in a circular or oval grave, laid on a rectangular mound of earth with a wooden stake fence, or placed on a scaffold. Important personal belongings, such as snowshoes, a gun and ammunition, and a pipe for smoking, were buried with the body. The drum and birch-bark canoe of the deceased were often hung in a nearby tree. After the burial, mourners expressed their anguish by grieving loudly. They then held a silent vigil for the rest of the day and night to keep the dead man's soul from returning to the family. After the funeral, the name of the deceased was never to be mentioned again. The eldest son usually succeeded his father as head of the household.

Getting Food

The Cree believed that the Creator—the supreme deity in their religion—had provided animals to them to give their flesh, fur, or feathers to hunters and fishermen. They further believed that plants and elements of the environment, such as the wind and water, were living spirits that could bring good weather for hunting, fishing, and gathering. The Cree also viewed themselves as part of nature, with their own complex and mysterious relationships with animals, plants, land, and weather.

The Cree hunted, fished, and gathered according to an annual cycle that followed the seasons. They trapped in the winter, hunted ducks and geese when these migratory birds were plentiful in the spring, fished in the summer, and hunted game in the fall. Armed with bows and arrows, spears, clubs, snares, and deadfalls,

The Cree traveled across many different areas to find food, including along shores of rivers and lakes.

Cree men were renowned as great hunters of caribou, elk, moose, and beavers. They also hunted bears when they could find them and snared rabbits when large game was scarce. The Cree relied heavily on fishing as well, especially for lake trout, pike, whitefish, and pickerel. Coastal people living near James Bay sometimes speared seals and beluga whales with harpoons for meat, fat, and skins. Sealskins were made into mittens and warm boots called mukluks.

The Plains Cree and a few southern groups rarely ate fish except when other foods were scarce. They caught a variety of game for meat or fur, including bears, beavers, prairie dogs, rabbits, squirrels, prairie chickens, foxes, coyotes, and wolves. However, they primarily hunted buffalo, which provided most of the meat in their diet. From the buffalo they also obtained skins for clothing and tipis, hair for twisting into rope, sinew for bowstrings and sewing thread, bone slivers for needles and arrowheads, teeth for jewelry, cartilage for boiling into glue, tails for fly swatters, skulls for lamps, and buffalo chips—or dried dung—for campfires.

Plains Cree hunters observed many customs to please the spirits and to ensure a good buffalo hunt. For example, every hunter carried his medicine pouch and hides painted with red stripes and dots. Once the scouts had located the herd, the Plains Cree hunted the buffalo in several ways. Sometimes, hunters approached downwind and then raced after the huge, shaggy animals on their horses. They galloped next to a buffalo—as close as they dared—and shot an arrow into its body from close range. Most hunters relied on bows and arrows because reloading a gun was slow and awkward on horseback. Some men also hunted with spears, which they plunged into the chests of the buffalo. Hunting in this manner called for great courage and skill.

The Plains Cree also stampeded buffalo into snowdrifts in the winter and into marshes in the summer, where the huge beasts foundered and could be easily shot. They also drove buffalo into pounds. Any man who wished to build a pound had to first have a vision in which he received supernatural assurances. The making of the buffalo pound was then overseen by

RECIPES

BAKED LAKE TROUT

INGREDIENTS

One 3- to 4-pound (1.4- to 1.8-kilogram) lake trout (or other fish)

3 tablespoons (44 milliliters) sunflower seed oil

Choice of herbs to taste (dill, parsley, and/or basil)

4 tablespoons (59 mL) fine cornmeal

Clean and split the trout, if necessary. Place in a greased baking pan, flesh side up, and sprinkle with sunflower seed oil, herbs, and cornmeal. Bake in oven at 350 degrees Fahrenheit (around 175 degrees Celsius) for 30 minutes. Serve with pea soup, wild rice, or mixed vegetables. Serves five to seven.

CREE-STYLE PEA SOUP

INGREDIENTS

2 cups (473 mL) dried peas, soaked

16 cups (3.8 liters) water

2.5 cups (591 mL) canned hominy

1 cup (236 mL) fresh celery leaves or
    2 teaspoons (10 mL) thyme

salt

pepper

Soak peas in water until soft. Place peas in a large pot with the other ingredients, except hominy. Simmer until the peas are tender but still firm. Add the hominy and stir until soup thickens. Serves five to seven.

just below the knee. Woodland Cree and Plains Cree women traditionally wore a wraparound skirt and a poncho-style shirt, although they later adopted the strap-and-sleeve dress. Some Plains Cree women also wore a kind of dress in which a single piece of buckskin was sewn with the seam on the side.

Many moccasins were decorated with patterns and warm fur.

Both men and women wore moccasins with fringed cuffs, which were often embroidered, quilled, or beaded with beautiful designs. Moccasins had special meaning to the Cree. As mentioned, during a wedding ceremony, the bride offered a pair of moccasins to her future husband so that he might walk long upon the earth. During the winter, the Plains Cree wore warm moccasins made of buffalo skin with the hair turned to the inside. The women also stuffed dried grass, prairie wool, or the longer hair from the buffalo's head into the moccasins for added protection against the cold.

Fur robes were worn by both men and women not only in cold weather but throughout the year. Cree men often wore robes made of woven strips of rabbit fur or moose or caribou hide with the hair left on for greater warmth. Some wore hooded parkas in a style similar to another Native group, the Inuit. The Plains Cree wore buffalo robes with the fur turned inside. The skin side was decorated with a strip of beadwork or adorned with two rows of painted figures. Warriors occasionally decorated their garments with pictures of battle heroics. Paintings of spirits were never featured on these robes, although they were sometimes depicted on ceremonial shirts.

Both men and women wore their hair hanging loose to the shoulders. However, some women tied their hair back or over the ears. Later they began to part their hair in the middle and braid it—only the very young and the very old did not braid their hair. The Plains Cree sometimes combed their hair with the rough side of a buffalo tongue and often painted a red line along the part. The Cree wrapped the lower part of the braid with strips of hide, fur, or sinew. Warriors occasionally cut the front part of their hair into bangs, stiffened them with grease, and combed them upward.

In the winter, the Cree wore caps made of rabbit or beaver fur, with the animal's head in front and tail in back. Eastern Cree women sometimes wore caps or peaked hoods of animal skin that were tied at the neck and often decorated with moose-hair embroidery or quillwork. Women later made these hats from wool that they adorned with beadwork and ribbons. Some Western Cree men wore peaked hats adorned with feathers. Cree men in the north also wore carved wooden goggles for protection against the glare of snow and ice. During the summer, Plains Cree men wore a sun visor made of a piece of stiff rawhide and ceremonial

Men and women would make warm coats with animal fur.

The People and Culture of the Cree

headdresses such as eagle feather bonnets and buffalo horn caps. In the winter, Plains Cree men also wore fur hats that covered the face except for the eyes and nose. These were made from the fur of many kinds of animals—coyote, rabbit, beaver, and even dog. They were shaped into a band with the animal's head in front and tail hanging in the back. They often were decorated with feathers or hornlike tufts of fur. During the winter, the Cree also slipped on warm fur mittens which they had made from rabbit fur or tanned animal skin.

Accessories

Women fashioned soft leather into drawstring bags and pouches for carrying personal objects, such as sewing materials, small tools, and tobacco. Plains Cree women wove bags from buffalo hair and fibers from the nettle plant. The Cree also made leather belts, sheaths for knives, and carrying straps, which were often decorated with quillwork.

Aside from bead or shell necklaces, the Cree did not wear much jewelry. The Western Cree often pierced their noses and inserted a bead. Sometimes, the Cree also wore ornaments in pierced ears, but usually they emphasized decoration on their clothing. However, the Plains Cree did come to favor long, white, tapered tubes made from seashells, called hair pipes, as ornaments. Both men and women wore hair pipes in strings at the sides of the face or as necklaces, earrings, or pendants. Cree men also liked to wear necklaces made of grizzly bear claws strung on a folded piece of skin or fur.

This drawing shows ancient Cree people sacrificing to their Creator, Kitchi-Kitchi-Manito.

*When you have a
special relationship with
the land ... you have a
special relationship with
the Creator himself.*

—Thomas Coon,
Mistissini Cree
tribe member

BELIEFS
OF THE
CREE

Although separated by distance, the different Cree bands were united by common beliefs and practices. They were, and still are, a deeply spiritual people who respect the earth and all living things around them. These are some of their beliefs.

The Cree celebrated rituals by wearing traditional dress and dancing.

their victory. The Cree enjoyed the Feasting or Greeting Dance when bands came together in the spring. To the rhythm of drums and rattles, they also had dances to celebrate animals such as the deer, caribou, and bear.

Among the Plains Cree, every band had at least one Askitci, or pipe stem bundle. The Cree believed the Great Spirit gave the pipe stem bundle to the first human being to help keep the peace. The bundle held the Sacred Pipe Stem. The pipe stem holds special significance for many Native American tribes. For the Cree, for example, there could be no violence in the presence of the Sacred Pipe Stem. When people quarreled, they had to make peace when the Askitci was presented to them—no matter how serious their argument. The Sacred Pipe Stem also helped to bring peace between warring tribes. Using the pipe to begin all rituals and sacred moments, men passed it in a clockwise direction, just as the sun moved in the sky. They made offerings and called upon the spirits, which they believed smoked with them and thus had to listen to their requests. Long strands of sweetgrass were plaited, and during

Many rituals were marked by the burning of sweetgrass.

ceremonies bits of the grass were broken off and burned on hot coals. The Cree believed that the fragrant smoke purified the people and their ritual.

The **Sun Dance** became the most important ceremony of the Plains Cree. In this sacred ceremony, young men pierced their bodies as a sacrifice to please the Creator. The Sun Dance was usually held just once a year, but another Sun Dance might be held for a special occasion. In this sacred gathering, everyone prayed and asked the spirits to heal a sick child or help with other difficulties. A Sun Dance could also be a social occasion, a time when old friends and distant family members came together again. People who had quarreled were expected to make up and become friends once again. However, Christian missionaries denounced the Sun Dance as a pagan ritual and had it outlawed. In 1885 an amendment of the Canadian

Indian Act made the Sun Dance a criminal offense. It remained illegal until 1951.

The religion of the Cree now blends traditional rituals and beliefs with Christianity. Many Cree devoutly attend Christian church services, but others also attend and take part in Sun Dances and summer **powwows**. A large number of Cree practice traditional healing rituals along with modern medicine.

The Story of the Bear, the Robin, and Fire

The Cree have many beliefs and stories about their ancestry. Here is a story about a small bird, which reflects the Cree view of nature and people:

> Many ages ago, there was only one fire in the world. It was kept burning by an old hunter who lived in a big forest. All the birds liked the fire because it was so warm. However, in that forest lived a bear who feared and hated the fire very much. The bear waited for his chance to get near enough to the fire to put it out, but he feared the old hunter's arrows and dared not approach when he was there.
>
> One day the old man became very ill. He could not tend the fire. When the bear saw that the old man was helpless and the fire was getting low, he rushed forward and trampled the last of the flames. Once the fire was out, the bear lumbered away.

The Cree shared many stories about animals, including the bear.

At the same time there was a little robin perched up in a tree. He saw what was happening, and he was very sad that the bear had destroyed the fire. He flew down to the ground and noticed that there was still a spark in the fire pit. The bird flapped his wings, and the fire flared up once again.

As he rekindled the flames, however, the robin did not notice that his feathers had also caught fire. He flew away, and wherever he rested, another fire started. So there came to be many fires throughout the land. And that is why the robin now has a red breast.

Sports and Fun

Cree children and adults enjoyed many athletic contests and games, which emphasized skill, intelligence, and strength. They played a kind of soccer on a field with two goals, each set about 100 feet (30.5 m) apart. Players tried to kick a head-sized ball made of buckskin and stuffed with animal hair across the opponent's goal. The main rule in this game was that no one was allowed to throw the ball. Some Cree people also played stickball, which was similar to modern-day **lacrosse**. In this game, they used rackets to fling a small ball into the opponent's goal.

Boys and men played many games related to hunting and warfare. In the otter hunting game, two men set up ten wooden figures of otters, each smaller than the other, and shot arrows at them. The object of the game was to shoot the smallest otter. In the caribou hunting game, boys and men used sticks to flip pebbles at a board set up about 6 to 10 feet (1.8 to 3 m) away. About 1 foot (0.3 m) long and 6 inches (15.2 cm) wide, the board represented a caribou. Sometimes, the Cree also used bows and arrows to shoot at this target.

In the goose hunting game, two boys sat in a blind, which was a place where hunters hid from approaching flocks of ducks and geese. Carrying goose feathers in their hands, two other boys approached from different directions. With flipping sticks, the two hunters then flung pebbles at the feathers. If one of his feathers was struck, the boy dropped it. Whoever hit the most feathers won this game. Related to this was the war game in which a man ran back and forth while the other

Children played with many toys, including slingshots.

warriors shot blunt arrows at him. Often played before going to war, this game helped boys and men practice their shooting skills and their ability to dodge arrows.

Children amused themselves with many kinds of handcrafted toys, such as small bows, slingshots, buzz toys, and carved wooden dolls. They played many games, such as hide-and-seek, tug-of-war, and a game called the square game. A square was made in the snow, and the person who was "it" stood in the center. The children called him "the cannibal." The other players stood in the corners. The object was to run from one corner to another without being touched by the cannibal. If the cannibal touched someone, that person then became "it."

Native American groups, including the Cree, played games such as cat's cradle.

Through the long winter, the Cree also played many games in the warmth of their tipis. In **taphan**, cone-shaped caribou bones were strung on a buckskin thong and tied to a bone or wooden striking pin. The object of the game was to toss the bones into the air and try to catch one of them on the striking pin. Bones tied farther away from the pin scored as many as ten points, while the closest bone scored only one point. People also liked to play hand games involving string figures, such as cat's cradle.

Like all groups of people, the Cree enjoyed celebrations, rituals, and games. These are examples of the Cree's most important and entertaining activities.

Men dance at the Rocky Boy's Reservation Powwow in Montana.

The Cree's beliefs, traditions, and lifestyles changed forever with the arrival of Europeans.

We never forget what has happened, but we cannot go back. Nor can we sit beside the trail.

—Chief Poundmaker

OVERCOMING HARDSHIPS

Life for the Cree began to change in the seventeenth and eighteenth centuries as more people moved into the territories the Cree called home. European traders first established contact with the Cree in the early 1600s, changing their lifestyle and communities in ways they could never have anticipated. Over the next few centuries, more immigrants crowded the region, forcing the Cree to endure hardships and loss of land in great amounts.

we do set to work, have so few cattle that one family goes to work, lots of others remain idle and we cannot put in much crop."

The Canadian government had agreed to provide livestock, seed grain, and agricultural implements, including plows and wagons. However, the Cree were given broken-down equipment and half-wild Montana cattle that could not be hitched to plows. Moreover, no mills were built in the region, where the Cree could store or market their wheat. Nonetheless, the Cree managed to increase their cattle herds and wheat farms until non-Natives argued that the government was helping

The People and Culture of the Cree

Caribou were one of many animals whose fur was made into clothing or traded for other goods.

the Cree too much. In 1889, such extensive restrictions were placed on the Cree that many were forced to give up cattle ranching and wheat farming.

While the Plains Cree struggled with starvation, the other Cree bands continued to face their own challenges. Christian missionaries who arrived in Ontario in the late 1800s converted a large number of Woodland Cree, although many continued to practice their traditional beliefs. The missionaries and traders also brought more diseases.

Moreover, the number of beaver and caribou, which had supplied furs and food, plunged dramatically in Ontario. The government also enforced game laws that limited Cree hunting of geese and ducks. Unable to provide game for their families, many Cree families starved.

The Woodland Cree also had to contend with an increasing number of settlers in their ancestral territory, along with damage from mining and railroads. In August 1905, tribal leaders signed Treaty Number 9 at Moose Factory. This treaty applied to the Cree living in Ontario. Each person in the band was paid $8 (about

Today, many Cree live for part of the year in tipis in the forest.

half his sentence, he was released due to poor health. Suffering from sickness and despair, he died the following year.

After Big Bear surrendered, his son Imasees led the rest of the Big Bear band into Montana, where Imasees changed his name to Little Bear. In 1896, the US government returned Little Bear and his "Canadian Indians" to Canada. However, a few weeks later, Little Bear and his band drifted back into Montana, where

The People and Culture of the Cree

they joined a small Ojibwe band led by Rocky Boy. In 1916, the US Congress authorized that a tract of abandoned military land be set aside as a reservation for the Little Bear/Rocky Boy band. The Rocky Boy's Reservation is located near the Canadian border, approximately 31 miles (50 km) south of Havre, Montana. It was the smallest and last reservation established in Montana. Descendants of those tribes still live on the reservation today.

Speaking Like the Cree

Cree is one of the most widely spoken Native languages in North America. In the **Algonquian** family of languages, it is closely related to the languages of the Montagnais and the Naskapi and the languages spoken by many other tribes, including the Abenaki, Arapaho, Cheyenne, Delaware, Micmac, Potawatomi, and Shawnee.

If you go to a James Bay community such as Chisasibi, you will hear people speaking Cree, a language that is perhaps older than the pyramids of Egypt. The language is still woven into the fabric of Cree culture. As Rodney A. Clifton wrote in *Semantic*

A Shoshone-Cree woman stays warm in a Hudson's Bay trade blanket. Many young people continue to celebrate the traditions of their people.

CHAPTER SIX

We must preserve our nationality for the youth of our future. The story should be written down and passed on.

—Louis Riel

THE NATION'S PRESENCE NOW

The descendants of the early Cree have maintained tradition throughout the centuries. Through careful preservation of their language and history by way of oral and written tradition, the Cree have become a popular and well-documented nation.

Population

As of 2015, there are approximately 317,000 Cree people officially registered in Canada. Most live in the provinces of Saskatchewan, Manitoba, and Alberta. However, these numbers do not take into consideration any Cree Nation members who are not Cree or who have blended ethnicities. Likewise, there are many "unofficial" bands or groups of Cree, such as the Métis, who are not included in the approximation. Most of the Métis are of Cree origin and speak "Michif," a unique French-Cree dialect that consists of French nouns and Cree verbs.

A Métis family, circa 1924

The People and Culture of the Cree

The Grand Council of the Crees

Unlike some Native groups, the Cree have always been a nation that has intermingled and connected throughout generations despite distance. A great unifying factor that speaks on behalf of Cree bands throughout Quebec is called the Grand Council of the Crees. This organization represents Quebec Cree nations and provides the nations a space to speak freely about concerns for their community and the nation as a whole. The Grand Council of the Crees has been instrumental to tackling political and environmental issues in the province, and remains a powerful voice for Quebec Cree rights and responsibilities.

Preserving Customs

Many Cree individuals and bands have preserved their traditional beliefs and customs. Large groups, such as the Plains, Woodland, Swampy, and Moose Cree, continue to live in Canada. Today, there are Cree reserves in Quebec, Ontario, Manitoba, Alberta, and Saskatchewan. There are nine Cree villages in Quebec, each with its own chief. A grand chief oversees these nine villages and the Grand Council of the Crees of Quebec. Altogether, these nine tribes have over ten thousand people living on their reserves. More people have left the reserves to find work or live life elsewhere. There are also many bands throughout Canada, including the Calling River People, Rabbit Skin People, Cree-Assiniboine, Touchwood Hills People, House People, Parklands People, Upstream People, and Downstream People. The Plains Cree also live on the Rocky Boy's Reservation in Chouteau and Hill counties in Montana.

The scenery around Cree territories continues to inspire and encourage generations.

Hunting, fishing, and gathering are still vitally important to the Cree. Many people live at least part of the year in the bush, following the traditional seasonal rounds for these outdoor activities. The Cree are also involved in several industries, notably mining, transportation, logging, and commercial fishing. Some Plains Cree raise horses, while Cree bands in Quebec

The People and Culture of the Cree

also operate a successful airline called Air Creebec. A number of Cree people work on the James Bay Hydroelectric Project in Quebec.

Many other people are employed in government programs on reserves throughout Canada. Others supplement their income making fine handicrafts, such as carved wooden figures, bark baskets, and buckskin moccasins. However, because of their relative isolation and lack of industry, unemployment remains high in Cree communities. Reserve life continues to be difficult. Many people live on welfare in government housing. They shop at a band store, send their children to a local school, and receive medical care at a nearby hospital, when necessary. With so few jobs available, many people have few opportunities on the reserve.

In recent years, Cree leaders have worked hard to achieve greater independence and control over their own services and resources. Many Cree now manage their own school system. Many Cree continue to speak their ancestral language, which is taught in these schools. However, people are still grappling with critical issues, such as the destruction of natural resources on their lands, the need for economic development, and unsteady relationships

Cree young people uphold the traditions of their ancestors.

*Instead of kids just
hearing about beads
and baskets and fringe ...
we present Native
American culture as a living
contemporary culture.*

—Buffy Sainte-Marie

FACES OF THE CREE NATION

Throughout the history of the Cree Nation, there have been many formidable and infamous people. Many of these men and women overcame struggle and hardship to shape the Cree Nation into what it is today. The list below features some of the most prominent figures in Cree history.

Big Bear (Mistihui'muskwa) (Plains Cree) (1825–1888), chief of an Ojibwe and Cree band, was born near Fort Carleton at Jackfish, Saskatchewan. By the 1870s, he became chief of a band of mixed Ojibwe and Cree people. In 1876, the Canadian government sent a Methodist missionary named George McDougall to invite chiefs of the Cree bands to treaty negotiations. While Big Bear led the largest band, he was not invited, possibly because McDougall intentionally forgot chiefs such as Big Bear who refused to convert to Christianity. Big Bear still went to the negotiations, but when he arrived the other chiefs had already signed the treaty

Big Bear

with the Canadian government. Big Bear at first opposed Treaty Number 6 and left without signing his name. At a council of two thousand Native peoples at Poundmaker's reserve in Cut Knife, he denounced the Canadian government and urged a united stand by his followers.

However, when his people faced starvation, Big Bear later conceded and signed the treaty. Yet, by 1885, conditions had still not

The People and Culture of the Cree

improved for Big Bear and his people, largely because the Canadian government failed to provide the band with adequate rations and land for a reserve. Big Bear then became one of the few Native people in western Canada to lead an uprising. His band joined Louis Riel's Métis in their 1885 struggle for territory along the North and South Saskatchewan Rivers.

Big Bear was forced to surrender when the Canadian government put down the rebellion. He was tried in a Canadian court and found guilty of treason. He was sentenced to three years of hard labor. After serving half his sentence, he was released in 1887 due to poor health. Suffering from sickness and despair, he died the following year, at the age of sixty-three.

Matthew Coon Come (1956–), Cree leader, grand chief of the Grand Council of the Crees, was born as a dog sled carrying his mother raced to a camp on his father's trap line. At age six, he was sent away to a boarding school. When he was sixteen, he read about threats to the ancestral land of his birth and became active in fighting for Native rights in Canada. He fought against the massive, multi-billion dollar hydroelectric project in northern Quebec. He read that one of the reservoirs was going to be built in his community and said, "Our home is going to be under water." He later graduated from Trent University in Ontario and studied law at McGill University before returning to his community to become deputy chief of the James Bay Cree People. He subsequently became chief of the group and has been reelected four times. In 1987 he was also first elected as grand chief of the Grand Council of the Crees and chair

Matthew Coon Come, grand chief of the Grand Council of the Crees, in 2014

of the Cree Regional Authority. In 1994 he received the Goldman Prize, which is considered the Nobel Prize of environmental awards. In 1995 he received the National Aboriginal Achievement Award, and in 1998 Trent University honored Coon Come with a Doctor of Laws Honoris Causa in recognition of his work. In 2000 he became the leader of all Native people in Canada when he was elected national chief of the Assembly of First Nations. His term finished in 2003.

He and his wife, Maryann Matoush, whom he married in 1976, have three daughters and two sons. Both he and his wife were taught by their parents how to live in the wilderness. Until they moved to Ottawa, they thrived on their territory in moose-hide coats and snowshoes. Over the course of his life, Matthew

Coon Come has perhaps been most noted for his international work in protecting the traditional ways of life of Native people. He continues to serve as the grand chief of the Grand Council of the Crees and the chair of the Cree Regional Authority.

Fine Day

Fine Day (Plains Cree) (circa 1850–ca.1935), war chief, was born of Cree parents in the Battle River area in Saskatchewan. As he grew up, he became a highly skilled warrior, shaman, and eventually war chief of the Poundmaker Cree band. During the North West Resistance in 1885, some of Poundmaker's followers raided the town of Battleford, Saskatchewan. Fearing retaliation from the Canadians, the warriors built a war lodge and sought Fine Day as their leader. Fine Day moved the band's camp to Cut Knife Hill. At dawn on May 2, Lieutenant Colonel Otter led 350 Canadian soldiers in an attack on the Cree camp. Fine Day and his warriors charged the Canadians from several directions. Otter thought they had five hundred warriors, but there were only fifty. Otter ordered a quick retreat of the Canadian Army at Cut Knife Hill. When Native resistance ended, Fine Day went to live with the

Piapot holds a rifle while wearing a coat and hat.

The People and Culture of the Cree

Sweetgrass Cree Band near Battleford and eventually became their chief. In 1934, when Fine Day was eighty-four, American anthropologist David Mandelbaum documented his recollections, some of which were published in a 1973 booklet entitled *My Cree People*. Fine Day's memoirs are a valuable firsthand account of Plains Cree life.

Piapot (Payepot, "One Who Knows the Secrets of the Sioux") (Plains Cree) (1816–1908), war chief, medicine man, and resistance leader, was raised by his grandmother after his parents died of smallpox. He and his grandmother were captured by the Sioux and lived with them for fourteen years until freed by a Cree war party. Because of his knowledge of Sioux customs and territory, Piapot became an important war chief in raids against Sioux bands.

In 1870, Piapot and his seven hundred warriors were soundly defeated by the Blackfeet. In 1875, he reluctantly signed Treaty Number 4, which ceded Cree territory in the Qu'appelle Valley of Manitoba. Piapot then moved his band farther west to what is now Saskatchewan. In 1882, in an act of defiance, Piapot's warriors yanked up survey stakes along a 30-mile (48.2 km) stretch of the Canadian Pacific Railway west of Moose Jaw. The following year, Piapot had his band set up their tipis in the path of the crew that was laying track. The Mounties (Canadian police) drove the Piapot and his people away, then knocked down their tipis. Piapot and his band eventually settled near Regina. Although he strongly resented the settling of Cree territory, Piapot kept his warriors out of the North West

Rebellion of 1885, unlike Big Bear and Poundmaker. Government officials removed Piapot as band leader after his people held a Sun Dance, which was forbidden under Canadian law. However, his people continued to regard him as their leader. He was also honored by Manitoba officials in 1901.

Poundmaker (Pitikwahanapiwiyin) (Plains Cree) (1842–1886), head chief, leader in the North West Rebellion of 1885, was born near Battleford, Saskatchewan, to a shaman father and a Métis mother. He was named for his special talent for making pounds, which were pens for trapping buffalo. When Poundmaker was about thirty years old, Crowfoot, chief of the Blackfeet, adopted him to replace one of his sons who had been killed in battle. A gifted orator and diplomat, Poundmaker counseled peaceful relations with settlers moving into Cree territory. In 1876, he convinced the Canadian government to add a "famine clause" to Treaty Number 6. Although Poundmaker still mistrusted the government, he finally signed the treaty at the urging of his followers. He settled with his people on a reserve near his birthplace, but when the government failed to supply his band with rations and farming tools, Poundmaker became fed up with government policies. In 1885, he allowed members of his band to become involved in resistance activities. Under the leadership of Fine Day, the band drove back a surprise attack by the Canadian Army at Cut Knife Hill. Fine Day then wanted to join the Métis in their resistance against the government, and he tried to lead the Plains Cree band to the Métis camp at Batoche. However,

The People and Culture of the Cree

Poundmaker with his family

Poundmaker delayed the band until the Métis had been defeated, and he then surrendered to Canadian authorities. Accused of treason, he was tried in Regina, Saskatchewan, and after two days the court found Poundmaker guilty. The judge sentenced him to three years' imprisonment in Manitoba's Stoney Mountain Penitentiary. He was released after less than a year due to poor health. Upon his release, he married Stony Woman, a woman much younger than he. Poundmaker and Stony

Woman then walked most of the 250 miles (402 km) to visit Crowfoot, his adoptive father and friend, because they had just one horse between them. Poundmaker died just four months after the time of his release.

Louis Riel (1844–1885), French-Canadian Métis leader, was born in present-day Manitoba. He studied law and for the priesthood, but he never finished his training in either profession. He was exiled from Canada in 1875 because of his role in the execution of a Canadian named Thomas Scott. Riel traveled to Indianapolis and Washington, DC, where he sought support from the United States government. When he returned to Quebec, he entered an asylum and began to refer to himself as "The Prophet of the New World." Riel believed that he had a calling to lead the Métis people of the Canadian northwest. Although only one-eighth Native, Riel became an ardent supporter of Native rights, especially Métis rights. In 1884, a small group of Métis asked him to present their grievances regarding land claims to the Canadian government. However, the government ignored these concerns until Riel established a provisional government, which quickly escalated tensions between the Métis and the federal authorities. In May 1885, government soldiers defeated the Métis in a four-day battle at Batoche, and two weeks later Riel surrendered to face charges of treason. On August 1, 1885, a jury found him guilty but recommended mercy. Nonetheless, Judge Hugh Richardson sentenced Riel to death. The court dismissed appeals, and a reexamination of Riel's mental state found him sane. He was hanged in Regina,

Louis Riel

Saskatchewan, on November 16, 1885. His execution was widely opposed in Quebec, where sympathy for the French-speaking Canadian was strong. A prolific writer of poetry and letters, Riel kept journals most of his life, many of which have been published. Ever year, on the third Monday of each February, the province of Manitoba recognizes Louis Riel Day in his memory.

Buffy Sainte-Marie is a contemporary singer and a member of the Cree tribe.

Buffy Sainte-Marie (1941–), folksinger and songwriter, was born in 1941 in Craven, Saskatchewan. She was orphaned as an infant and raised by a Micmac couple in Massachusetts. She studied Eastern philosophy in college but had long wanted to become a singer and musician.

She began playing the guitar and writing songs when she was sixteen. Inspired by the warm reception to her work, she moved to New York City and began singing in many folk clubs in Greenwich Village. She

The People and Culture of the Cree

was soon offered a recording contract with Vanguard Records. Over the years, she had many hit songs, such as "Universal Soldier" and "Until It's Time for You to Go." Her 1992 recording, entitled *Confidence and Likely Stories*, emphasized string music and complex rhythms that were markedly different from her earlier folk songs. A new album, *Power in the Blood*, was released in 2015. Much of her work is concerned with Native issues and rights. She has contributed writings to numerous Native American publications, and she is the author of *Nokosis and the Magic Hat* (1986), a children's book set on a reservation.

Wandering Spirit (Kapapamahchakwew) (Plains Cree) (1845–1885), war chief of the Big Bear band, was born near Jackfish Lake, Saskatchewan. When he was still a young man, Wandering Spirit distinguished himself as a warrior. During his life, he killed fifteen Blackfeet warriors, who were the Cree's traditional enemy. After he became war chief of the Big Bear nation in the late 1870s, Wandering Spirit remained hostile toward settlers, especially for their role in killing off the buffalo. In 1880, on a hunting expedition in Montana, he met Louis Riel, who tried to convince Wandering Spirit that the Cree and the Métis should become allies in driving settlers from the Great Plains and establishing their own independent nation. In 1885, Wandering Spirit again voiced his anger with Thomas Quinn, the Native agent at Frog Lake, Saskatchewan. Quinn had a strict "no work, no food" policy toward the Cree. On April 2, Wandering Spirit led his warriors into Frog Lake, where he shot Quinn, and his followers then killed eight non-Natives and one Métis. Wandering Spirit surrendered at Fort Pitt in early July and was tried for murder. He had no lawyer to defend him, and he admitted killing Quinn but refused to offer any explanation.

On September 24, 1885, Judge Charles Rouleau stated, "The sentence of the court is that you, Wandering Spirit, be taken back to jail till Friday the 27th day of November, and then be taken to the scaffold and there be hanged by the neck until you are dead; and may God have mercy on your soul." The day before his execution, Wandering Spirit told a journalist that he did not fear death, but did not want to enter the afterlife with a ball and chain on his ankle. He was greatly relieved to learn that it would be removed before he was hanged. Wandering Spirit was hanged on November 27, 1885, at Battleford, Saskatchewan. According to Cree legend, Wandering Spirit did not sing his death song as he stood on the scaffold, but a love song for his wife.

Each man and woman in the Cree Nation has a special story. These men and women were integral to the survival of the Cree people and helped pave the way for future generations of Cree. Without them, the Cree Nation would be a very different group today. It is through their struggle and determination that the tribes have continued to remain essential parts of North America's history.

CHRONOLOGY

1611 Henry Hudson trades with the Cree while exploring James Bay.

ca. 1650 The Jesuits are the first Europeans to document contact with the Cree.

1670–1688 The Cree become active traders of European goods after the Hudson's Bay Company is established near their territory.

1780–1782 Smallpox epidemic rages through the tribes in the Hudson Bay area.

1821 The North West Company merges with the Hudson's Bay Company, which then monopolizes the fur trade.

1842 Poundmaker is born near Battleford, Saskatchewan.

1870 The Canadian government purchases land from the Hudson's Bay Company, and the homeland of the Cree and other Native people becomes the Canadian frontier.

1871–1921 Cree reluctantly sign the eleven Numbered Treaties with the Canadian government.

1876 Poundmaker becomes chief of a Cree band. Treaty Number 6 is signed, in which the Plains Cree submit to many government demands in exchange for reserve lands, rations, services, and equipment.

1879 Poundmaker accepts a small reserve west of Battleford, in present-day west-central Saskatchewan.

1885 Louis Riel leads the Métis in an uprising against the Canadian government after Métis land claims are ignored. The Métis are defeated at Batoche, and Riel is found guilty of treason and hanged.

1886 Poundmaker dies on July 4, four months after being released from jail after serving less than a year of his sentence.

1899 Treaty Number 8 is signed by the Cree and Chipewyan peoples of Fort McMurray, exchanging hunting and trapping lands for reserves, tools, and payments.

1905 The province of Saskatchewan is formed by combining the Northwest Territory provisional districts of Assiniboia, Saskatchewan, and Athabaska.

1958 The Federation of Saskatchewan Indians is formed by Native groups in Saskatchewan.

1965 On May 13, Judge J. M. Policha rules that under the "Medicine Chest" provision of Treaty Number 6, the

Canadian government must provide health care for all registered Native people in Saskatchewan living on and off reserves.

1971 The James Bay Hydroelectric Project is announced by Quebec premier Robert Bourassa. Cree and Inuit leaders protest in Quebec courts.

1974 A Quebec Supreme Court injunction briefly stops the massive James Bay Hydroelectric Project in northern Quebec from flooding large areas of Inuit and Cree territory, but when the ruling is overturned a week later, the project goes ahead as planned.

1996 Chief Poundmaker Historical Centre and Teepee Village is opened on the Poundmaker Cree Nation reserve.

1998 On February 5, the Poundmaker Cree Nation is awarded a parcel of land by the Saskatchewan provincial government under the Saskatchewan Treaty Land Entitlement Framework Agreement.

2001 The 125th anniversary of the adoption of Treaty Number 6, which Poundmaker signed, is observed. A powwow is held at Duck Lake to mark the occasion.

2002 The Cree and Hydro Québec agree to terms for a new generator in the James Bay Hyrdroelectric Project.

GLOSSARY

adze A tool with a sharp blade that is used to shape wood.

ahtchak A person's soul.

Algonquian A group, or family, of more than twenty languages that is one of the most widespread and commonly spoken throughout North America. Many Native American tribes speak Algonquian languages, including the Cree.

Atayohkanak Lesser spirits of animals and plants that served as intermediaries between people and the Creator, Kitchi-Kitchi-Manito.

babiche A cord made from rawhide used in making shoes.

breechcloth A rectangular piece of buckskin worn by men; also called breechclout.

cradleboard A wooden board used to carry a baby.

Great Plains A vast area of prairie stretching across the central part of North America from Texas to Canada.

indigenous Native to a place or region.

Jesuit A priest in the Society of Jesus, a Roman Catholic order founded by Saint Ignatius Loyola in 1534.

Kitchi-Kitchi-Manito Meaning "Great-Great Spirit," the Cree creator.

lacrosse A modern sport based on a stickball game that was popular among Native American tribes living in eastern North America.

Matchi-Manito Meaning "Evil Spirit," resembling the devil, to whom the Cree made sacrifices.

Métis A person of mixed Euro-American (usually French or English) and Native American (often Cree) ancestry, especially in western Canada.

michwaup A summer tipi made with cedar or spruce poles and a canvas covering.

moccasins Soft leather shoes often decorated with brightly colored quillwork or beads.

muhtukan A rectangular winter home made of logs and sod.

muskeg Northern boggy land, typically with spruce trees and sphagnum moss.

nomad A person or group of people that moves from place to place.

Numbered Treaties A series of treaties between Native peoples across Canada and the government.

pemmican A food made from lean meat that is dried, pounded down, and mixed with fat that has been melted.

portage To carry or transport goods or boats overland from one body of water to another.

powwow A modern Native American gathering featuring dancers and drum groups.

quillwork Decorative embroidery patterns created with the quills of porcupines or birds.

reserves Parcels of land set aside for Native peoples and held in trust by the Canadian government. Called reservations in the United States.

Sacred Pipe Stem An object that had great significance to the Cree people. It was used in ceremonies and to settle disputes.

shaman A holy person responsible for the spiritual and physical healing of tribal members. Also called healer or medicine man.

spirit helper In Native American culture, an apparition, usually in animal form, that appears in dreams or visions and guides an individual in matters concerning hunting, battle, or love.

Sun Dance A sacred ceremony held every summer in which the Plains Cree give thanks for their good fortune.

sweat lodge A dome-shaped hut covered with animal skins in which individuals purified themselves.

taphan A winter game played indoors with caribou bones and a bone or wooden striking pin.

tipi A cone-shaped home made of poles covered with animal skins.

travois A sled-like carrier made from two long poles tied together to make an A-shaped frame pulled by dogs and later horses to transport tipis and belongings from one place to another.

vision quest A ritual in which individuals went off alone to fast and pray with hopes of having a vision in which their spirit helper is revealed to them.

wigwam A domed house made of a wooden frame covered with bark or animal skins.

Wisahketchak Meaning "Trickster Spirit," who could bring good luck or misfortune to people.

BIBLIOGRAPHY

Boyden, Joseph. *Louis Riel and Gabriel Dumont*. Extraordinary Canadians. Toronto, ON: Penguin Canada, 2010.

Carlson, Hans. *Home Is the Hunter: The James Bay Cree and Their Land*. Nature, History, Society. Seattle, WA: University of Washington Press, 2009.

Cuthand, Doug. *Askiwina: A Cree World*. Regina, SK: Coteau Books, 2007.

Daschuk, James. *Clearing the Plains: Disease, Politics of Starvation, and the Loss of Aboriginal Life*. Regina, SK: University of Regina Press, 2013.

Ellis, Deborah. *Looks Like Daylight: Voices of Indigenous Kids*. Toronto, ON: Groundwood Books, 2013.

Howard, Heather A., and Craig Proulx, eds. *Aboriginal Peoples in Canadian Cities: Transformers and Continuities*. Indigenous Studies. Waterloo, ON: Wilfrid Laurier University Press, 2011.

Mcleod, Neal. *Cree Narrative Memory: From Treaties to Contemporary Times*. Saskatoon, SK: Purich Publishing Ltd., 2007.

Niezen, Ronald. *Defending the Land: Sovereignty and Forest Life in James Bay Cree Society*. 2nd ed. Cultural Survival Studies in Ethnicity and Change. New York: Pearson, 2008.

Ratt, Solomon. *Woods Cree Stories*. Regina, SK: University of Regina Press, 2014.

Smallman, Shawn. *Dangerous Spirits: The Windigo in Myth and History*. Victoria, BC: Heritage House, 2014.

St-Onge, Nicole, Carolyn Podruchny, and Brenda Macdougall, eds. *Contours of a People: Metis Family, Mobility, and History*. New Directions in Native American Studies. Norman, OK: University of Oklahoma Press, 2014.

Townsend, Kenneth W. *First Americans: A History of Native Peoples*. New York: Pearson, 2012.

Watetch, Abel. *Payepot and His People*. Regina, SK: University of Regina Press, 2007.

Wiebe, Rudy. *Big Bear*. Extraordinary Canadians. Toronto, ON: Penguin Canada, 2008.

Wilson, Ian M., ed. *Thirty Years Among the Indians of the Northwest: The Personal Experiences of Father Constantine Scollen*. Kindle edition. Cheyenne, WY: Wyoming State Library, 2014.

FURTHER INFORMATION

Want to know more about the Cree? Check out these websites, videos, and organizations.

Websites

Cree Cultural Institute

www.creeculturalinstitute.ca/en

This website displays information about the Cree Cultural Institute, a place that preserves and promotes Cree culture. It has many pages of information as well as a virtual tour.

Cree Nation Arts and Crafts Association

www.cnaca.ca

This website gives information on different arts and crafts events happening in North America.

Encyclopedia Britannica: Cree

www.britannica.com/EBchecked/topic/142354/Cree

This website offers a detailed history of the Cree.

Grand Council of the Crees

www.gcc.ca

This is the official website of the political body of the Cree tribes in Quebec, Canada.

Videos

Big Bear's Story

www.youtube.com/watch?v=K1Cpz1HZ8F0

This brief video tells the story of Big Bear, one of the Cree's Plains chiefs.

CrashCourse: The Black Legend, Native Americans, and Spaniards

www.youtube.com/watch?v=6E9WU9TGrec

This website explains what it was like for Native Americans when they first encountered Europeans. It is engaging and informative, with many animations.

Organizations

Chisasibi Mandow Agency

PO Box 720
Chisasibi, QC J0M 1E0
Canada
(819) 855-3373
www.mandow.ca

Cree Nation of Eastmain

76 Nouchimi, PO Box 90

Eastmain, QC J0M 1W0

Canada

(819) 977-0211

www.eastmain.ca

Cree Nation of Mistissini

187 Main Street

Mistissini, QC G0W 1C0

Canada

(418) 923-3461

www.mistissini.ca/en/home.html

Cree Nation of Wemindji

6 Paint Hills

Wemindji, QC J0M 1L0

Canada

(819) 978-0264

www.wemindji.ca

Lucky Man Cree Nation

103-103A Packham Avenue

Saskatoon, SK S7N 4K4

Canada

(306) 374-2828

Mikisew Cree First Nation
Box 90
Ft. Chipewyan, AB T0P 1B0
Canada
(780) 697-3740
mikisewcree.ca

Norway House Cree Nation
PO Box 250
Norway House, MB R0B 1B0
Canada
(204) 359-6721
www.nhcn.ca

Oujè-Bougoumou
203 Opemiska Meskino
Oujè-Bougoumou, QC G0W 3C0
Canada
(888) 745-3905

Rocky Boy's Reservation
Chippewa-Cree Tribe
PO Box 544
Box Elder, MT 59521
United States
(406) 395-5705

Tataskweyak Cree Nation

General Delivery
Split Lake, MB R0B 1P0
Canada
(204) 342-2045
tataskweyak.mb.ca

Waswanipi Cree First Nation

1 Chief Louis R. Gull Street
Waswanipi, QC, J0Y 3C0
Canada
(819) 753-2587
www.waswanipi.com

Woodland Cree First Nation

General Delivery
Cadotte Lake, AB T0H 0N0
Canada
(780) 629-3803
www.woodlandcree.net

York Factory First Nation

General Delivery
York Landing, MB R0B 2B0
Canada
(204) 341-2180
www.yorkfactoryfirstnation.ca

INDEX

ABOUT THE AUTHOR

Raymond Bial has published more than eighty books—most of them photography books—during his career. His photo-essays for children include *Corn Belt Harvest*, *Amish Home*, *Frontier Home*, *Shaker Home*, *The Underground Railroad*, *Portrait of a Farm Family*, *With Needle and Thread: A Book About Quilts*, *Mist Over the Mountains: Appalachia and Its People*, *Cajun Home*, and *Where Lincoln Walked*.

As with his other work, Bial's deep feeling for his subjects is evident in both the text and illustrations. He travels to tribal cultural centers, photographing homes, artifacts, and surroundings and learning firsthand about the national lifeways of these peoples.

The emeritus director of a small college library in the Midwest, he lives with his wife and three children in Urbana, Illinois.